Gratitude Journal
12 weeks

www.gratitudeandmore.ca

Copyright © 2016 by Leah Strange

All rights reserved.

This book may not be re-sold. No part of this book may be used, reproduced or transmitted by any means without written permission by the author.

Having enjoyed journaling for many years, I wanted something more than blank space to write out my gratitude list. This journal was created to help you *want* to journal every day.

Journaling can be very transformative. With this in mind, you are prompted with daily questions—questions that have an impact on your physical, emotional and spiritual well-being.

Each day is two pages, one with daily prompts and one lined page for any additional writing. There is also a Weekly Check-In page that allows you to review the previous week and set your intention for the coming days.

I hope you enjoy your journey over the next twelve weeks. A grateful life is a happy life.

For more information on the wide variety of journals we offer, visit us at www.gratitudeandmore.ca

Journal—see where it takes you!

Leah

To thine own self be true. (William Shakespeare)

Date:	Mood/Happiness Scale (1-10): AM PM
Did I spend time with those I love?	Was I fully present?

I am grateful for:

How did I enrich my spiritual life?	How did I move my body today?

Did I nourish my body and drink enough water?

What do I need to work on?	Did I express myself creatively?
Did I spend responsibly?	Today's highlights:
Was I generous and kind? (to me too)	

Dare to be remarkable!

Date:	Mood/Happiness Scale (1-10): AM PM
Did I spend time with those I love?	Was I fully present?
I am grateful for:	
How did I enrich my spiritual life?	How did I move my body today?
Did I nourish my body and drink enough water?	
What do I need to work on?	Did I express myself creatively?
Did I spend responsibly?	Today's highlights:
Was I generous and kind? (to me too)	

Abundance flows through me. I am a channel for the Universe.

Date:	Mood/Happiness Scale (1-10): AM PM
Did I spend time with those I love?	Was I fully present?
I am grateful for:	
How did I enrich my spiritual life?	How did I move my body today?
Did I nourish my body and drink enough water?	
What do I need to work on?	Did I express myself creatively?
Did I spend responsibly?	Today's highlights:
Was I generous and kind? (to me too)	

Rise! Do not shrink.

Date:	Mood/Happiness Scale (1-10): AM PM
Did I spend time with those I love?	Was I fully present?

I am grateful for:

How did I enrich my spiritual life?	How did I move my body today?

Did I nourish my body and drink enough water?

What do I need to work on?	Did I express myself creatively?

Did I spend responsibly?	Today's highlights:
Was I generous and kind? (to me too)	

You are worthy. You are important. You are loved.

REVIEW OF LAST WEEK

How balanced was my time? (work/family/Me)	Did I get outside every day for fresh air?
Did I have the support I needed?	Did I ask for help when I needed it?

Did I remember my intentions from last week?

Did I spend enough time being unplugged?

I am proud that I....

Notes:

WEEKLY CHECK-IN

My Intention for Next Week:

I would like to:

Experience…

Let go of…

Feel…

Learn to…

Stop…

I want more of…	I want less of…

Date:	Mood/Happiness Scale (1-10): AM　　　　　　　　PM
Did I spend time with those I love?	Was I fully present?
I am grateful for:	
How did I enrich my spiritual life?	How did I move my body today?
Did I nourish my body and drink enough water?	
What do I need to work on?	Did I express myself creatively?
Did I spend responsibly?	Today's highlights:
Was I generous and kind? (to me too)	

The Universe is conspiring with you, never against you.

Date:	Mood/Happiness Scale (1-10): AM PM
Did I spend time with those I love?	Was I fully present?
I am grateful for:	
How did I enrich my spiritual life?	How did I move my body today?
Did I nourish my body and drink enough water?	
What do I need to work on?	Did I express myself creatively?
Did I spend responsibly?	Today's highlights:
Was I generous and kind? (to me too)	

All that I seek is already within me.

Date:	Mood/Happiness Scale (1-10): AM PM
Did I spend time with those I love?	Was I fully present?

I am grateful for:

How did I enrich my spiritual life?	How did I move my body today?

Did I nourish my body and drink enough water?

What do I need to work on?	Did I express myself creatively?
Did I spend responsibly?	Today's highlights:
Was I generous and kind? (to me too)	

I am guided by my intention. I am open to the Universe.

Date:	Mood/Happiness Scale (1-10): AM　　　　　　　　　　PM
Did I spend time with those I love?	Was I fully present?
I am grateful for:	
How did I enrich my spiritual life?	How did I move my body today?
Did I nourish my body and drink enough water?	
What do I need to work on?	Did I express myself creatively?
Did I spend responsibly?	Today's highlights:
Was I generous and kind? (to me too)	

I am unlimited. My life is filled with abundance.

Date:	Mood/Happiness Scale (1-10): AM PM
Did I spend time with those I love?	Was I fully present?
I am grateful for:	
How did I enrich my spiritual life?	How did I move my body today?
Did I nourish my body and drink enough water?	
What do I need to work on?	Did I express myself creatively?
Did I spend responsibly?	Today's highlights:
Was I generous and kind? (to me too)	

I have freed myself from fear and self-doubt.

Date:	Mood/Happiness Scale (1-10): AM PM
Did I spend time with those I love?	Was I fully present?

I am grateful for:

How did I enrich my spiritual life?	How did I move my body today?

Did I nourish my body and drink enough water?

What do I need to work on?	Did I express myself creatively?
Did I spend responsibly?	Today's highlights:
Was I generous and kind? (to me too)	

I am in sync. I flow with the river of life.

Date:	Mood/Happiness Scale (1-10): AM PM
Did I spend time with those I love?	Was I fully present?
I am grateful for:	
How did I enrich my spiritual life?	How did I move my body today?
Did I nourish my body and drink enough water?	
What do I need to work on?	Did I express myself creatively?
Did I spend responsibly?	Today's highlights:
Was I generous and kind? (to me too)	

I choose to release fear, anger, hurt and resentment.

REVIEW OF LAST WEEK

How balanced was my time? (work/family/Me)	Did I get outside every day for fresh air?
Did I have the support I needed?	Did I ask for help when I needed it?

Did I remember my intentions from last week?

Did I spend enough time being unplugged?

I am proud that I....

Notes:

WEEKLY CHECK-IN

My Intention for Next Week:

I would like to:

Experience...

Let go of...

Feel...

Learn to...

Stop...

I want more of...	I want less of...

Date:	Mood/Happiness Scale (1-10): AM PM
Did I spend time with those I love?	Was I fully present?
I am grateful for:	
How did I enrich my spiritual life?	How did I move my body today?
Did I nourish my body and drink enough water?	
What do I need to work on?	Did I express myself creatively?
Did I spend responsibly?	Today's highlights:
Was I generous and kind? (to me too)	

I forgive others; I love myself and deserve the freedom it brings.

Date:	Mood/Happiness Scale (1-10): AM PM
Did I spend time with those I love?	Was I fully present?
I am grateful for:	
How did I enrich my spiritual life?	How did I move my body today?
Did I nourish my body and drink enough water?	
What do I need to work on?	Did I express myself creatively?
Did I spend responsibly?	Today's highlights:
Was I generous and kind? (to me too)	

How do you act authentically?

Date:	Mood/Happiness Scale (1-10): AM PM
Did I spend time with those I love?	Was I fully present?
I am grateful for:	
How did I enrich my spiritual life?	How did I move my body today?
Did I nourish my body and drink enough water?	
What do I need to work on?	Did I express myself creatively?
Did I spend responsibly?	Today's highlights:
Was I generous and kind? (to me too)	

I am open to new experiences and new people.

Date:	Mood/Happiness Scale (1-10): AM PM
Did I spend time with those I love?	Was I fully present?
I am grateful for:	
How did I enrich my spiritual life?	How did I move my body today?
Did I nourish my body and drink enough water?	
What do I need to work on?	Did I express myself creatively?
Did I spend responsibly?	Today's highlights:
Was I generous and kind? (to me too)	

Be still and know that I am God. (Psalm 46:10)

Date:	Mood/Happiness Scale (1-10): AM　　　　　　　　PM
Did I spend time with those I love?	Was I fully present?

I am grateful for:

How did I enrich my spiritual life?	How did I move my body today?

Did I nourish my body and drink enough water?

What do I need to work on?	Did I express myself creatively?

Did I spend responsibly?	Today's highlights:
Was I generous and kind? (to me too)	

I am patient, tolerant and filled with compassion.

Date:	Mood/Happiness Scale (1-10): AM PM
Did I spend time with those I love?	Was I fully present?
I am grateful for:	
How did I enrich my spiritual life?	How did I move my body today?
Did I nourish my body and drink enough water?	
What do I need to work on?	Did I express myself creatively?
Did I spend responsibly?	Today's highlights:
Was I generous and kind? (to me too)	

I love every cell of my beautiful self.

Date:	Mood/Happiness Scale (1-10): AM PM
Did I spend time with those I love?	Was I fully present?

I am grateful for:

How did I enrich my spiritual life?	How did I move my body today?

Did I nourish my body and drink enough water?

What do I need to work on?	Did I express myself creatively?
Did I spend responsibly?	Today's highlights:
Was I generous and kind? (to me too)	

I am protected and safe.

REVIEW OF LAST WEEK

How balanced was my time? (work/family/Me)	Did I get outside every day for fresh air?
Did I have the support I needed?	Did I ask for help when I needed it?

Did I remember my intentions from last week?

Did I spend enough time being unplugged?

I am proud that I....

Notes:

WEEKLY CHECK-IN

My Intention for Next Week:

I would like to:

Experience…

Let go of…

Feel…

Learn to…

Stop…

I want more of…	I want less of…

Date:	Mood/Happiness Scale (1-10): AM PM
Did I spend time with those I love?	Was I fully present?
I am grateful for:	
How did I enrich my spiritual life?	How did I move my body today?
Did I nourish my body and drink enough water?	
What do I need to work on?	Did I express myself creatively?
Did I spend responsibly?	Today's highlights:
Was I generous and kind? (to me too)	

My body is strong and supports me in all I do.

Date:	Mood/Happiness Scale (1-10): AM　　　　　　　　　PM
Did I spend time with those I love?	Was I fully present?
I am grateful for:	
How did I enrich my spiritual life?	How did I move my body today?
Did I nourish my body and drink enough water?	
What do I need to work on?	Did I express myself creatively?
Did I spend responsibly?	Today's highlights:
Was I generous and kind? (to me too)	

My life is unfolding with ease.

Date:	Mood/Happiness Scale (1-10): AM 　　　　　　　　PM
Did I spend time with those I love?	Was I fully present?
I am grateful for:	
How did I enrich my spiritual life?	How did I move my body today?
Did I nourish my body and drink enough water?	
What do I need to work on?	Did I express myself creatively?
Did I spend responsibly?	Today's highlights:
Was I generous and kind? (to me too)	

My days are filled with excitement and love.

Date:	Mood/Happiness Scale (1-10): AM　　　　　　　　　　　PM
Did I spend time with those I love?	Was I fully present?

I am grateful for:

How did I enrich my spiritual life?	How did I move my body today?

Did I nourish my body and drink enough water?

What do I need to work on?	Did I express myself creatively?
Did I spend responsibly?	Today's highlights:
Was I generous and kind? (to me too)	

Serenity is not the absence of conflict, but the ability to cope with it.

Date:	Mood/Happiness Scale (1-10): AM　　　　　　　　　PM
Did I spend time with those I love?	Was I fully present?

I am grateful for:

How did I enrich my spiritual life?	How did I move my body today?
Did I nourish my body and drink enough water?	
What do I need to work on?	Did I express myself creatively?
Did I spend responsibly?	Today's highlights:
Was I generous and kind? (to me too)	

At the center of your being you have the answer; you know who you are and you know what you want. (Lao Tzu)

Date:	Mood/Happiness Scale (1-10): AM PM
Did I spend time with those I love?	Was I fully present?
I am grateful for:	
How did I enrich my spiritual life?	How did I move my body today?
Did I nourish my body and drink enough water?	
What do I need to work on?	Did I express myself creatively?
Did I spend responsibly?	Today's highlights:
Was I generous and kind? (to me too)	

Everyone has a story. It's not how you tell it. It's how you live it.

Date:	Mood/Happiness Scale (1-10): AM PM
Did I spend time with those I love?	Was I fully present?

I am grateful for:

How did I enrich my spiritual life?	How did I move my body today?

Did I nourish my body and drink enough water?

What do I need to work on?	Did I express myself creatively?
Did I spend responsibly?	Today's highlights:
Was I generous and kind? (to me too)	

The two most important days in your life are the day you were born and the day you find out why. (Mark Twain)

REVIEW OF LAST WEEK

How balanced was my time? (work/family/Me)	Did I get outside every day for fresh air?
Did I have the support I needed?	Did I ask for help when I needed it?

Did I remember my intentions from last week?

Did I spend enough time being unplugged?

I am proud that I....

Notes:

WEEKLY CHECK-IN

My Intention for Next Week:

I would like to:

Experience…

Let go of…

Feel…

Learn to…

Stop…

I want more of…	I want less of…

Date:	Mood/Happiness Scale (1-10): AM PM
Did I spend time with those I love?	Was I fully present?
I am grateful for:	
How did I enrich my spiritual life?	How did I move my body today?
Did I nourish my body and drink enough water?	
What do I need to work on?	Did I express myself creatively?
Did I spend responsibly?	Today's highlights:
Was I generous and kind? (to me too)	

The task ahead of us is never as great as the Power behind us.
(Ralph Waldo Emerson)

Date:	Mood/Happiness Scale (1-10): AM PM
Did I spend time with those I love?	Was I fully present?

I am grateful for:

How did I enrich my spiritual life?	How did I move my body today?

Did I nourish my body and drink enough water?

What do I need to work on?	Did I express myself creatively?
Did I spend responsibly?	Today's highlights:
Was I generous and kind? (to me too)	

It's all an inside job.

Date:	Mood/Happiness Scale (1-10): AM PM
Did I spend time with those I love?	Was I fully present?

I am grateful for:

How did I enrich my spiritual life?	How did I move my body today?
Did I nourish my body and drink enough water?	
What do I need to work on?	Did I express myself creatively?
Did I spend responsibly?	Today's highlights:
Was I generous and kind? (to me too)	

Do you want to be right or do you want to be happy?

Date:	Mood/Happiness Scale (1-10): AM PM
Did I spend time with those I love?	Was I fully present?
I am grateful for:	
How did I enrich my spiritual life?	How did I move my body today?
Did I nourish my body and drink enough water?	
What do I need to work on?	Did I express myself creatively?
Did I spend responsibly?	Today's highlights:
Was I generous and kind? (to me too)	

Each new day offers twenty-four hours of possibility and moves you forward on your path.

Date:	Mood/Happiness Scale (1-10): AM PM
Did I spend time with those I love?	Was I fully present?
I am grateful for:	
How did I enrich my spiritual life?	How did I move my body today?
Did I nourish my body and drink enough water?	
What do I need to work on?	Did I express myself creatively?
Did I spend responsibly?	Today's highlights:
Was I generous and kind? (to me too)	

Each day may not be good, but there is good in every day. (Alice Earle)

Date:	Mood/Happiness Scale (1-10): AM PM
Did I spend time with those I love?	Was I fully present?

I am grateful for:

How did I enrich my spiritual life?	How did I move my body today?
Did I nourish my body and drink enough water?	
What do I need to work on?	Did I express myself creatively?
Did I spend responsibly?	Today's highlights:
Was I generous and kind? (to me too)	

The first step towards getting somewhere is to decide that you are not going to stay where you are.

Date:	Mood/Happiness Scale (1-10): AM　　　　　　　　　PM
Did I spend time with those I love?	Was I fully present?
I am grateful for:	
How did I enrich my spiritual life?	How did I move my body today?
Did I nourish my body and drink enough water?	
What do I need to work on?	Did I express myself creatively?
Did I spend responsibly?	Today's highlights:
Was I generous and kind? (to me too)	

It's not about being the best, it's about being better than you were yesterday.

REVIEW OF LAST WEEK

How balanced was my time? (work/family/Me)	Did I get outside every day for fresh air?
Did I have the support I needed?	Did I ask for help when I needed it?

Did I remember my intentions from last week?

Did I spend enough time being unplugged?

I am proud that I....

Notes:

WEEKLY CHECK-IN

My Intention for Next Week:

I would like to:

Experience...

Let go of...

Feel...

Learn to...

Stop...

I want more of...	I want less of...

Date:	Mood/Happiness Scale (1-10): AM PM
Did I spend time with those I love?	Was I fully present?
I am grateful for:	
How did I enrich my spiritual life?	How did I move my body today?
Did I nourish my body and drink enough water?	
What do I need to work on?	Did I express myself creatively?
Did I spend responsibly?	Today's highlights:
Was I generous and kind? (to me too)	

The mind is slow in unlearning what it has been long in learning. (Seneca)

Date:	Mood/Happiness Scale (1-10): AM PM
Did I spend time with those I love?	Was I fully present?
I am grateful for:	
How did I enrich my spiritual life?	How did I move my body today?
Did I nourish my body and drink enough water?	
What do I need to work on?	Did I express myself creatively?
Did I spend responsibly?	Today's highlights:
Was I generous and kind? (to me too)	

*Be ready at any moment to sacrifice what you are
for what you could become. (Charles Dubois)*

Date:	Mood/Happiness Scale (1-10): AM PM
Did I spend time with those I love?	Was I fully present?

I am grateful for:

How did I enrich my spiritual life?	How did I move my body today?

Did I nourish my body and drink enough water?

What do I need to work on?	Did I express myself creatively?
Did I spend responsibly?	Today's highlights:
Was I generous and kind? (to me too)	

When one is willing and eager, the gods join in. (Aeschylus)

Date:	Mood/Happiness Scale (1-10): AM PM
Did I spend time with those I love?	Was I fully present?

I am grateful for:

How did I enrich my spiritual life?	How did I move my body today?

Did I nourish my body and drink enough water?

What do I need to work on?	Did I express myself creatively?

Did I spend responsibly?	Today's highlights:
Was I generous and kind? (to me too)	

*The real voyage of discovery consists not in seeing new landscapes,
but in having new eyes. (Marcel Proust)*

Date:	Mood/Happiness Scale (1-10): AM PM
Did I spend time with those I love?	Was I fully present?

I am grateful for:

How did I enrich my spiritual life?	How did I move my body today?
Did I nourish my body and drink enough water?	
What do I need to work on?	Did I express myself creatively?
Did I spend responsibly?	Today's highlights:
Was I generous and kind? (to me too)	

There is no way to happiness. Happiness is the way. (Thich Nhat Hanh)

Date:	Mood/Happiness Scale (1-10): AM PM
Did I spend time with those I love?	Was I fully present? |■
I am grateful for:	

How did I enrich my spiritual life?	How did I move my body today?
Did I nourish my body and drink enough water?	
What do I need to work on?	Did I express myself creatively?
Did I spend responsibly?	Today's highlights:
Was I generous and kind? (to me too)	

Be the change you want to see in the world. (Mahatma Gandhi)

Date:	Mood/Happiness Scale (1-10): AM　　　　　　　　PM
Did I spend time with those I love?	Was I fully present?
I am grateful for:	
How did I enrich my spiritual life?	How did I move my body today?
Did I nourish my body and drink enough water?	
What do I need to work on?	Did I express myself creatively?
Did I spend responsibly?	Today's highlights:
Was I generous and kind? (to me too)	

If the only prayer you ever say in your whole life is "thank you", that would suffice. (Meister Eckhart)

REVIEW OF LAST WEEK

How balanced was my time? (work/family/Me)	Did I get outside every day for fresh air?
Did I have the support I needed?	Did I ask for help when I needed it?

Did I remember my intentions from last week?

Did I spend enough time being unplugged?

I am proud that I....

Notes:

WEEKLY CHECK-IN

My Intention for Next Week:

I would like to:

Experience...

Let go of...

Feel...

Learn to...

Stop...

I want more of...	I want less of...

Date:	Mood/Happiness Scale (1-10): AM　　　　　　　　　　PM
Did I spend time with those I love?	Was I fully present?

I am grateful for:

How did I enrich my spiritual life?	How did I move my body today?

Did I nourish my body and drink enough water?

What do I need to work on?	Did I express myself creatively?
Did I spend responsibly?	Today's highlights:
Was I generous and kind? (to me too)	

Believe in miracles, but do the footwork.

Date:	Mood/Happiness Scale (1-10): AM　　　　　　　　　　　PM
Did I spend time with those I love?	Was I fully present?

I am grateful for:

How did I enrich my spiritual life?	How did I move my body today?

Did I nourish my body and drink enough water?

What do I need to work on?	Did I express myself creatively?
Did I spend responsibly?	Today's highlights:
Was I generous and kind? (to me too)	

Leave room—life's most treasured moments often come unannounced.

Date:	Mood/Happiness Scale (1-10): AM PM
Did I spend time with those I love?	Was I fully present?
I am grateful for:	
How did I enrich my spiritual life?	How did I move my body today?
Did I nourish my body and drink enough water?	
What do I need to work on?	Did I express myself creatively?
Did I spend responsibly?	Today's highlights:
Was I generous and kind? (to me too)	

Be willing to accept a temporary inconvenience for a permanent improvement.

Date:	Mood/Happiness Scale (1-10): AM　　　　　　　　PM
Did I spend time with those I love?	Was I fully present?

I am grateful for:

How did I enrich my spiritual life?	How did I move my body today?

Did I nourish my body and drink enough water?

What do I need to work on?	Did I express myself creatively?
Did I spend responsibly?	Today's highlights:
Was I generous and kind? (to me too)	

Seek respect rather than popularity.

Date:	Mood/Happiness Scale (1-10): AM PM
Did I spend time with those I love?	Was I fully present?
I am grateful for:	
How did I enrich my spiritual life?	How did I move my body today?
Did I nourish my body and drink enough water?	
What do I need to work on?	Did I express myself creatively?
Did I spend responsibly?	Today's highlights:
Was I generous and kind? (to me too)	

Is what you're doing today getting you closer to where you want to be tomorrow?

Date:	Mood/Happiness Scale (1-10): AM PM
Did I spend time with those I love?	Was I fully present?

I am grateful for:

How did I enrich my spiritual life?	How did I move my body today?
Did I nourish my body and drink enough water?	
What do I need to work on?	Did I express myself creatively?
Did I spend responsibly?	Today's highlights:
Was I generous and kind? (to me too)	

Belief is simply acceptance without proof.

Date:	Mood/Happiness Scale (1-10): AM PM
Did I spend time with those I love?	Was I fully present?

I am grateful for:

How did I enrich my spiritual life?	How did I move my body today?

Did I nourish my body and drink enough water?

What do I need to work on?	Did I express myself creatively?
Did I spend responsibly?	Today's highlights:
Was I generous and kind? (to me too)	

The only people with whom you should try to get even with are those who have helped you. (John E. Southard)

REVIEW OF LAST WEEK

How balanced was my time? (work/family/Me)	Did I get outside every day for fresh air?
Did I have the support I needed?	Did I ask for help when I needed it?

Did I remember my intentions from last week?

Did I spend enough time being unplugged?

I am proud that I....

Notes:

WEEKLY CHECK-IN

My Intention for Next Week:

I would like to:

Experience…

Let go of…

Feel…

Learn to…

Stop…

I want more of…	I want less of…

Date:	Mood/Happiness Scale (1-10): AM PM
Did I spend time with those I love?	Was I fully present?

I am grateful for:

How did I enrich my spiritual life?	How did I move my body today?

Did I nourish my body and drink enough water?

What do I need to work on?	Did I express myself creatively?
Did I spend responsibly?	Today's highlights:
Was I generous and kind? (to me too)	

Failure isn't being knocked down—it's staying down.

Date:	Mood/Happiness Scale (1-10): AM PM
Did I spend time with those I love?	Was I fully present?
I am grateful for:	
How did I enrich my spiritual life?	How did I move my body today?
Did I nourish my body and drink enough water?	
What do I need to work on?	Did I express myself creatively?
Did I spend responsibly?	Today's highlights:
Was I generous and kind? (to me too)	

What do you dream of when no one is watching?

Date:	Mood/Happiness Scale (1-10): AM　　　　　　　　PM
Did I spend time with those I love?	Was I fully present?
I am grateful for:	
How did I enrich my spiritual life?	How did I move my body today?
Did I nourish my body and drink enough water?	
What do I need to work on?	Did I express myself creatively?
Did I spend responsibly?	Today's highlights:
Was I generous and kind? (to me too)	

The more we resist, the more stuck we become.

Date:	Mood/Happiness Scale (1-10): AM PM
Did I spend time with those I love?	Was I fully present?

I am grateful for:

How did I enrich my spiritual life?	How did I move my body today?

Did I nourish my body and drink enough water?

What do I need to work on?	Did I express myself creatively?
Did I spend responsibly?	Today's highlights:
Was I generous and kind? (to me too)	

Start each day with a sense of possibility.

Date:	Mood/Happiness Scale (1-10): AM PM
Did I spend time with those I love?	Was I fully present?

I am grateful for:

How did I enrich my spiritual life?	How did I move my body today?

Did I nourish my body and drink enough water?

What do I need to work on?	Did I express myself creatively?

Did I spend responsibly?	Today's highlights:
Was I generous and kind? (to me too)	

The same boiling water that softens the potato hardens the egg. It's about what you're made of, not the circumstances. (Unknown)

Date:	Mood/Happiness Scale (1-10): AM　　　　　　　　PM
Did I spend time with those I love?	Was I fully present?
I am grateful for:	
How did I enrich my spiritual life?	How did I move my body today?
Did I nourish my body and drink enough water?	
What do I need to work on?	Did I express myself creatively?
Did I spend responsibly?	Today's highlights:
Was I generous and kind? (to me too)	

We know what we are but know not what we may be. (William Shakespeare)

Date:	Mood/Happiness Scale (1-10): AM PM
Did I spend time with those I love?	Was I fully present?
I am grateful for:	
How did I enrich my spiritual life?	How did I move my body today?
Did I nourish my body and drink enough water?	
What do I need to work on?	Did I express myself creatively?
Did I spend responsibly?	Today's highlights:
Was I generous and kind? (to me too)	

I care not so much what I am to others as what I am to myself.
(Michel Eyquem de Montaigne)

REVIEW OF LAST WEEK

How balanced was my time? (work/family/Me)	Did I get outside every day for fresh air?
Did I have the support I needed?	Did I ask for help when I needed it?

Did I remember my intentions from last week?

Did I spend enough time being unplugged?

I am proud that I....

Notes:

WEEKLY CHECK-IN

My Intention for Next Week:

I would like to:

Experience...

Let go of...

Feel...

Learn to...

Stop...

I want more of...	I want less of...

Date:	Mood/Happiness Scale (1-10): AM　　　　　　　　　PM
Did I spend time with those I love?	Was I fully present?

I am grateful for:

How did I enrich my spiritual life?	How did I move my body today?

Did I nourish my body and drink enough water?

What do I need to work on?	Did I express myself creatively?
Did I spend responsibly?	Today's highlights:
Was I generous and kind? (to me too)	

We are what we do, not what we say we do.

Date:	Mood/Happiness Scale (1-10): AM PM
Did I spend time with those I love?	Was I fully present?

I am grateful for:

How did I enrich my spiritual life?	How did I move my body today?

Did I nourish my body and drink enough water?

What do I need to work on?	Did I express myself creatively?
Did I spend responsibly?	Today's highlights:
Was I generous and kind? (to me too)	

Let your faith be bigger than your fear.

Date:	Mood/Happiness Scale (1-10): AM PM
Did I spend time with those I love?	Was I fully present?
I am grateful for:	
How did I enrich my spiritual life?	How did I move my body today?
Did I nourish my body and drink enough water?	
What do I need to work on?	Did I express myself creatively?
Did I spend responsibly?	Today's highlights:
Was I generous and kind? (to me too)	

Do the next right thing.

Date:	Mood/Happiness Scale (1-10): AM PM
Did I spend time with those I love?	Was I fully present?

I am grateful for:

How did I enrich my spiritual life?	How did I move my body today?

Did I nourish my body and drink enough water?

What do I need to work on?	Did I express myself creatively?
Did I spend responsibly?	Today's highlights:
Was I generous and kind? (to me too)	

Don't complain about the things you're not willing to change.

Date:	Mood/Happiness Scale (1-10): AM PM
Did I spend time with those I love?	Was I fully present?
I am grateful for:	
How did I enrich my spiritual life?	How did I move my body today?
Did I nourish my body and drink enough water?	
What do I need to work on?	Did I express myself creatively?
Did I spend responsibly?	Today's highlights:
Was I generous and kind? (to me too)	

You are not here to figure out your life, you are here to create it.

Date:	Mood/Happiness Scale (1-10): AM PM
Did I spend time with those I love?	Was I fully present?

I am grateful for:

How did I enrich my spiritual life?	How did I move my body today?

Did I nourish my body and drink enough water?

What do I need to work on?	Did I express myself creatively?

Did I spend responsibly?	Today's highlights:
Was I generous and kind? (to me too)	

*Stop worrying about what can go wrong and
get excited about what can go right.*

Date:	Mood/Happiness Scale (1-10): AM　　　　　　　　　PM
Did I spend time with those I love?	Was I fully present?

I am grateful for:

How did I enrich my spiritual life?	How did I move my body today?

Did I nourish my body and drink enough water?

What do I need to work on?	Did I express myself creatively?
Did I spend responsibly?	Today's highlights:
Was I generous and kind? (to me too)	

If there is no change, there is no change.

REVIEW OF LAST WEEK

How balanced was my time? (work/family/Me)	Did I get outside every day for fresh air?
Did I have the support I needed?	Did I ask for help when I needed it?

Did I remember my intentions from last week?

Did I spend enough time being unplugged?

I am proud that I....

Notes:

WEEKLY CHECK-IN

My Intention for Next Week:

I would like to:

Experience...

Let go of...

Feel...

Learn to...

Stop...

I want more of...	I want less of...

Date:	Mood/Happiness Scale (1-10): AM PM
Did I spend time with those I love?	Was I fully present?

I am grateful for:

How did I enrich my spiritual life?	How did I move my body today?

Did I nourish my body and drink enough water?

What do I need to work on?	Did I express myself creatively?
Did I spend responsibly?	Today's highlights:
Was I generous and kind? (to me too)	

Life: It's the greatest journey you will ever be on.

Date:	Mood/Happiness Scale (1-10): AM PM
Did I spend time with those I love?	Was I fully present?

I am grateful for:

How did I enrich my spiritual life?	How did I move my body today?
Did I nourish my body and drink enough water?	
What do I need to work on?	Did I express myself creatively?
Did I spend responsibly?	Today's highlights:
Was I generous and kind? (to me too)	

You are today where your thoughts have brought you; you will be tomorrow where your thoughts take you. (James Allen)

Date:	Mood/Happiness Scale (1-10): AM PM
Did I spend time with those I love?	Was I fully present?

I am grateful for:

How did I enrich my spiritual life?	How did I move my body today?
Did I nourish my body and drink enough water?	
What do I need to work on?	Did I express myself creatively?
Did I spend responsibly?	Today's highlights:
Was I generous and kind? (to me too)	

Most people are about as happy as they make up their minds to be.
(Abraham Lincoln)

Date:	Mood/Happiness Scale (1-10): AM PM
Did I spend time with those I love?	Was I fully present?

I am grateful for:

How did I enrich my spiritual life?	How did I move my body today?
Did I nourish my body and drink enough water?	
What do I need to work on?	Did I express myself creatively?
Did I spend responsibly?	Today's highlights:
Was I generous and kind? (to me too)	

The love of oneself is the beginning of a lifelong romance. (Oscar Wilde)

Date:	Mood/Happiness Scale (1-10): AM　　　　　　　　　PM
Did I spend time with those I love?	Was I fully present?

I am grateful for:

How did I enrich my spiritual life?	How did I move my body today?
Did I nourish my body and drink enough water?	
What do I need to work on?	Did I express myself creatively?
Did I spend responsibly?	Today's highlights:
Was I generous and kind? (to me too)	

To accomplish great things, we must not only act, but also dream, not only plan, but also believe. (Anatole France)

Date:	Mood/Happiness Scale (1-10): AM PM
Did I spend time with those I love?	Was I fully present?

I am grateful for:

How did I enrich my spiritual life?	How did I move my body today?

Did I nourish my body and drink enough water?

What do I need to work on?	Did I express myself creatively?
Did I spend responsibly?	Today's highlights:
Was I generous and kind? (to me too)	

Let yourself be silently drawn by the stronger pull of what you really love.
(Rumi)

Date:	Mood/Happiness Scale (1-10): AM　　　　　　　　　PM
Did I spend time with those I love?	Was I fully present?

I am grateful for:

How did I enrich my spiritual life?	How did I move my body today?

Did I nourish my body and drink enough water?

What do I need to work on?	Did I express myself creatively?
Did I spend responsibly?	Today's highlights:
Was I generous and kind? (to me too)	

Start by doing what is necessary; then do what's possible; and suddenly you are doing the impossible. (St. Francis of Assisi)

REVIEW OF LAST WEEK

How balanced was my time? (work/family/Me)	Did I get outside every day for fresh air?
Did I have the support I needed?	Did I ask for help when I needed it?

Did I remember my intentions from last week?

Did I spend enough time being unplugged?

I am proud that I....

Notes:

WEEKLY CHECK-IN

My Intention for Next Week:

I would like to:

Experience...

Let go of...

Feel...

Learn to...

Stop...

I want more of...	I want less of...

Date:	Mood/Happiness Scale (1-10): AM　　　　　　　　　PM
Did I spend time with those I love?	Was I fully present?

I am grateful for:

How did I enrich my spiritual life?	How did I move my body today?
Did I nourish my body and drink enough water?	
What do I need to work on?	Did I express myself creatively?
Did I spend responsibly?	Today's highlights:
Was I generous and kind? (to me too)	

Maybe it's about unbecoming everything that isn't really you, so you can be who you were meant to be in the first place. (Unknown)

Date:	Mood/Happiness Scale (1-10): AM PM
Did I spend time with those I love?	Was I fully present?

I am grateful for:

How did I enrich my spiritual life?	How did I move my body today?

Did I nourish my body and drink enough water?

What do I need to work on?	Did I express myself creatively?
Did I spend responsibly?	Today's highlights:
Was I generous and kind? (to me too)	

Life is really simple, but we insist on making it complicated. (Confucius)

Date:	Mood/Happiness Scale (1-10): AM PM
Did I spend time with those I love?	Was I fully present?

I am grateful for:

How did I enrich my spiritual life?	How did I move my body today?

Did I nourish my body and drink enough water?

What do I need to work on?	Did I express myself creatively?
Did I spend responsibly?	Today's highlights:
Was I generous and kind? (to me too)	

Very little is needed to make a happy life; it is all within yourself, in your way of thinking. (Marcus Aurelius)

Date:	Mood/Happiness Scale (1-10): AM PM
Did I spend time with those I love?	Was I fully present?

I am grateful for:

How did I enrich my spiritual life?	How did I move my body today?
Did I nourish my body and drink enough water?	
What do I need to work on?	Did I express myself creatively?
Did I spend responsibly?	Today's highlights:
Was I generous and kind? (to me too)	

Let your dreams be bigger than your fears, your actions louder than your words and your faith stronger than your feelings. (Unknown)

Date:	Mood/Happiness Scale (1-10): AM PM
Did I spend time with those I love?	Was I fully present?

I am grateful for:

How did I enrich my spiritual life?	How did I move my body today?

Did I nourish my body and drink enough water?

What do I need to work on?	Did I express myself creatively?

Did I spend responsibly?	Today's highlights:
Was I generous and kind? (to me too)	

I am only one, but I am one. I cannot do everything, but I can do something and I will not let what I cannot do interfere with what I can do. (Edward Everett Hale)

Date:	Mood/Happiness Scale (1-10): AM PM
Did I spend time with those I love?	Was I fully present?
I am grateful for:	
How did I enrich my spiritual life?	How did I move my body today?
Did I nourish my body and drink enough water?	
What do I need to work on?	Did I express myself creatively?
Did I spend responsibly? Was I generous and kind? (to me too)	Today's highlights:

Tension is who you think you should be. Relaxation is who you are.
(Chinese Proverb)

Date:	Mood/Happiness Scale (1-10): AM PM
Did I spend time with those I love?	Was I fully present?
I am grateful for:	
How did I enrich my spiritual life?	How did I move my body today?
Did I nourish my body and drink enough water?	
What do I need to work on?	Did I express myself creatively?
Did I spend responsibly?	Today's highlights:
Was I generous and kind? (to me too)	

Go confidently in the direction of your dreams and live the life you have imagined. (Henry David Thoreau)

REVIEW OF LAST WEEK	
How balanced was my time? (work/family/Me)	Did I get outside every day for fresh air?
Did I have the support I needed?	Did I ask for help when I needed it?
Did I remember my intentions from last week?	
Did I spend enough time being unplugged?	
I am proud that I....	
Notes:	

WEEKLY CHECK-IN

My Intention for Next Week:

I would like to:

Experience...

Let go of...

Feel...

Learn to...

Stop...

I want more of...	I want less of...

Date:	Mood/Happiness Scale (1-10): AM PM
Did I spend time with those I love?	Was I fully present?

I am grateful for:

How did I enrich my spiritual life?	How did I move my body today?
Did I nourish my body and drink enough water?	
What do I need to work on?	Did I express myself creatively?
Did I spend responsibly?	Today's highlights:
Was I generous and kind? (to me too)	

You yourself, as much as anybody in the entire universe deserve your love and affection. (Buddha)

Date:	Mood/Happiness Scale (1-10): AM PM
Did I spend time with those I love?	Was I fully present?
I am grateful for:	
How did I enrich my spiritual life?	How did I move my body today?
Did I nourish my body and drink enough water?	
What do I need to work on?	Did I express myself creatively?
Did I spend responsibly?	Today's highlights:
Was I generous and kind? (to me too)	

Habit is a cable; we weave a thread of it each day, and at last we cannot break it. (Horace Mann)

Date:	Mood/Happiness Scale (1-10): AM PM
Did I spend time with those I love?	Was I fully present?

I am grateful for:

How did I enrich my spiritual life?	How did I move my body today?
Did I nourish my body and drink enough water?	
What do I need to work on?	Did I express myself creatively?
Did I spend responsibly?	Today's highlights:
Was I generous and kind? (to me too)	

If a man wants his dreams to come true, he must wake them up. (Unknown)

Date:	Mood/Happiness Scale (1-10): AM PM
Did I spend time with those I love?	Was I fully present?

I am grateful for:

How did I enrich my spiritual life?	How did I move my body today?

Did I nourish my body and drink enough water?

What do I need to work on?	Did I express myself creatively?
Did I spend responsibly?	Today's highlights:
Was I generous and kind? (to me too)	

A comfort zone is a beautiful place, but nothing ever grows there.

Date:	Mood/Happiness Scale (1-10): AM PM
Did I spend time with those I love?	Was I fully present?
I am grateful for:	
How did I enrich my spiritual life?	How did I move my body today?
Did I nourish my body and drink enough water?	
What do I need to work on?	Did I express myself creatively?
Did I spend responsibly?	Today's highlights:
Was I generous and kind? (to me too)	

There is only one way to happiness and that is to cease worrying about things which are beyond the power of our will. (Epictetus)

Date:	Mood/Happiness Scale (1-10): AM PM
Did I spend time with those I love?	Was I fully present?

I am grateful for:

How did I enrich my spiritual life?	How did I move my body today?

Did I nourish my body and drink enough water?

What do I need to work on?	Did I express myself creatively?
Did I spend responsibly?	Today's highlights:
Was I generous and kind? (to me too)	

True happiness is...to enjoy the present, without anxious dependence upon the future. (Lucius Annaeus Seneca)

Date:	Mood/Happiness Scale (1-10): AM PM
Did I spend time with those I love?	Was I fully present?
I am grateful for:	
How did I enrich my spiritual life?	How did I move my body today?
Did I nourish my body and drink enough water?	
What do I need to work on?	Did I express myself creatively?
Did I spend responsibly?	Today's highlights:
Was I generous and kind? (to me too)	

Happiness is the consequence of personal effort...you have to participate relentlessly in the manifestations of your own blessings. (Elizabeth Gilbert)

REVIEW OF LAST WEEK

How balanced was my time? (work/family/Me)	Did I get outside every day for fresh air?
Did I have the support I needed?	Did I ask for help when I needed it?

Did I remember my intentions from last week?

Did I spend enough time being unplugged?

I am proud that I....

Notes:

Made in the USA
Charleston, SC
30 October 2016